A Walk with Christ

By
Raymond Lunt

Poetry, Meditations and character reflections

British Library Cataloguing in Publication Data.
A catalogue record for this book is available from the British Library

ISBN 978 0 86071 671 6

Joint Publication with

MOORLEYS
Print & Publishing
tel: 0115 932 0643 web: www.moorleys.co.uk

CONTENTS

INTRODUCTION

Life often includes a variety of journeys. Some are recurring and routine, others have a particular significance. A pilgrimage to the Holy Land remains vivid in my mind, with its powerful Biblical connections and a sense of walking in the steps of Jesus Christ, recalling some of the places and stories in the gospels.

But as well as the pilgrimage itself, I also remember some of the people with whom it was shared and their personal stories of their walk with Christ.

The Christian life is a pilgrimage shared with Christ and others on the Way. The title of this book and its content seek to capture something of a pilgrimage experience in poetry, meditation and character reflection.

I am grateful to those who helped me on the Christian way so many years ago; to those with whom I have shared the experience in various parts of the country; to my wife Gwen with whom the journey has been shared, and who has presented some of the material in this book as we have visited churches and groups.

Ray and Gwen continue to present this and other material at venues and church events and groups. If you would like to invite Ray and Gwen please email them at rayandgwen@btinternet.com

The Author

Raymond Lunt was a Chartered Accountant in professional practice for a number of years before entering the Methodist Church Ministry. He is now a Supernumerary Minister (retired) and lives in Derbyshire.

Through Advent To Christmas

YOUR GOD IS COMING
An Advent Poem

"Your God is coming."
A prophet's cry
Through distant sky –
A new age is beginning.
Across the mountains sound the news
To each new generation;
Cry hope and peace, for your God comes
To bring again salvation.

"Your God is coming."
A virgin birth
Unique on earth:
A new age is beginning.
The breaking news, God's great surprise,
The greatest gift is given;
The Son of God now Son of man;
In a child, earth touched with heaven.

"Your God is coming."
The angels cry
In starlit sky;
A new age is beginning.
Over shepherds' fields a heavenly choir
Sing: "To God on high be glory."
In Bethlehem, the House of Bread,
Is born a sacramental story.

"Your God is coming."
Some will adore
And some ignore
The new age now beginning.
Beside a lake; down city street;
Love's touch and word is found;
'Til from a cross salvation flows
Upon the blood drenched ground.

"Your God is coming."
Coming today
Down your way;
A new age is beginning.
To heal the brokenness and hurt;
And birth new worlds of love;
God's kingdom now is here on earth
As it is in heaven above.

"Your God is coming."
The Spirit burns
As Christ returns,
The end times consummating.
Jesus of cradle, the Christ of the cross,
Returns with power and glory;
But the promise of amazing grace
Remains the final story.

MY MESSENGER

The messenger - bringer of pleasure or of pain -
Promising unanticipated joy;
Carrier of heartache and of tears.
How often has the future been
For ever changed, in a moment,
When my messenger comes.

The messenger - bringer of pleasure and of pain -
The letter announcing an engagement;
The call to say a grandchild has been born;
The visit of a friend so long forgotten,
Reborn by time and circumstance;
The legacy that was never dreamed of;
The promotion you did not think would come.
The future for ever changed
By my messenger.

The messenger - bringer of pleasure and of pain -
Carrier of tears and overwhelming hurt.
The news from Afghanistan is not good
And now the dread is devastation
As life so promising lies buried in the dust
Of all the evils of an age of war.
No father for a new born babe;
No son to welcome home once more;
Only a wreath of flowers born of tears;
The future for ever changed
By my messenger.

Long ago my messenger came
With hope for a better world
Where peace and love would blossom
On a landscape withered by human wickedness.
My messenger would come to bring good news;
A new dawn, a new age,
An advent hope and harmony
For a world broken by evil, pain and doubt.
Good news of a future birthed by grace,
And alive with the music of light
And songs of overwhelming love.
The future for ever changed
By my messenger.

The messenger came and brought good news
Wrapped in confusion, promises and surprise.
Came to a village girl – pure, but promised to a man;
To you will be born a child from God;
Gift of grace to a world needing mercy.
From the womb of a country girl
God will come with mercy to the world.
Power will face the gentleness of God
Whose voice once spoke creation
And now breathes new creation.
The future for ever changed
By my messenger.

HOPE

Hope is a light in a dark and fearful place;
a familiar sound breaking the silence of inner dread.
Hope is a smile from a body wracked with pain;
a rose that blossoms on a thorny bush.

Hope is a signpost on the road of faith.
Hope is a touch, a word that speaks of healing and of peace.
Hope lies beyond the horizon of our dreams
and sees a vision greater than our reason can embrace.

Hope came to exiles with a dream of home – the grand return to
their Jerusalem.
Hope came to earth in a virgin birth;
an eternal word made flesh.
Hope extended its arms to those for whom all hope had gone.
Hope agonised with suffering on a cross and cried forgiveness.
Hope lay buried in a Jesus tomb until an Easter Christ arose
and now lives on for all who will receive Him
and welcome His new future as their own.

Hope, born of crisis, ends with glory.

MARY'S "YES" OR "WHY ME?"

(I attended an Advent Quiet Day at a URC Church in Sutton Coldfield. The theme was "Mary's Yes", with three sessions introduced by the leader and plenty of time for personal reflection. During one of those periods I wrote the following piece. Mary is speaking.)

Why me?
God almighty; holy; eternal.
Why me?
To be the host of Your presence;
The mother of Your Son;
The carer for Your – Your humanity?

It isn't possible – for me or You!

It isn't possible for <u>me</u>!
I am not worthy. I am not important.
I am simplicity wrapped in a shawl of common things.
All I have is my home; my friends;
and the dignity of my untouched purity.
It isn't possible for <u>me</u>!

It isn't possible for <u>You</u>!
That You should have a human face
and take the risk of birth
by bursting in upon my deepest secret
kept for the man of my dreams.
That You should stoop so low;
that I should look into the human face of a child
and see the very face of God.

My life is simple; my dream uncomplicated.
But now you want to change all that
and make me part of Your divine plan
big enough to change the world.

Why me?
I am nothing. You are everything.
I do not see beyond Nazareth.
You ask me to see eternity.
"No", would be personally comfortable for me.
"Yes" means I recognise God's moment for the world.

Is there a choice?

(November 2002)

BETHLEHEM

Bethlehem, such a small town;
Little houses, narrow streets, a market square;
Oh! and the inn - not four star by any means.
Bethlehem, such a small town,
But with a noble history -
"Royal David's City".

Here, years ago, three brave men,
Under cover of darkness,
Stole secretly through the ranks
Of powerful Philistine warriors,
Simply to draw water from a well.
Why risk so much?
It was water for their king.
Royal David was their noble king,
And they loved him.
Bethlehem, such a small town
With such a large history
Of sacrificial love.

One day someone from this royal line
Will come to rule again with noble enterprise.

Joseph, descendent of David, comes with Mary,
Through the ranks of guards and soldiers
To a silent manger underneath the inn,
And there in humble birth
Eternal sacrificial love is born.
There, earth is touched with heaven
In the human face of God.

AS A CHILD
Meditation

In the weakness of a child, Lord,
I see the strength of Your love.
In the conception of a virgin
I believe in Your divine humanness.
In the poverty of a manger
I am aware of the depth of Your grace,
Embracing the soul of humanity
In great diversity, united to You.
The baby in the manger makes it plain;
God is interested in me, and invites my love.

Lord, through the eyes of a child
You view a world in need of Your healing.
In the cry of a child
You feel the pain of a world in need of love.
With the hands of a child
You grasp a whole universe with hope.
With the touch of a child
You share Your presence and Your peace.
Through the helplessness of a child
You invite my complete dependence on You.
I rejoice in the blessed gift of the Christ child
Breaking in on my world with new possibilities.

Encounters on the Way

FOLLOW ME

I met Jesus by the shores
Of the Lake of Galilee,
When he said, "My friend, today,
Will you come and follow me?"

I met Jesus late at night
When I saw Him secretly;
He talked of being born again,
And said, "Will you follow me."

I met Jesus at the city gate,
His face I could not see;
But then he healed my blinded eyes
And He said, "Come, follow me."

I met Jesus in our house
In the village of Bethany.
I bathed His sore and tired feet,
And He said, "Come, follow me."

I met Jesus one afternoon
When I'd climbed into a tree.
He looked, and with His searching eyes,
Said "Come down and follow me."

I met Jesus nailed to a cross
On the hill of Calvary.
I heard His word of forgiving love
As he said, "Sinner, follow me."

I met Jesus on a dusty road
When His light surrounded me,
I could not struggle any more
For His voice said, "Follow me".

I meet Jesus every day
At home with the family,
For we've let Him come into our hearts
When he said, "Friends, follow me."

Will you meet Jesus here today,
He calls you longingly,
And says, "My friend, whoever you are,
You, too, can follow me."

(This poem could be presented using different character voices.)

WATER INTO WINE

At a wedding feast in Cana
When a bridegroom gave a shout,
The celebration faltered
When the stock of wine ran out.
Your mother came to You and said,
"My son, what can be done?"
And You pondered for a moment:
Had God's time for You begun?
You noticed there some water pots
Servants used for washing feet.
"Fill them to the brim", You said,
"Then people's needs we'll meet.
Now pour out into goblets
As the people sit and dine."
And by Your hand of blessing
The ordinary water
Became the smoothest wine.

Water into wine, Lord,
New life You will provide;
Water into wine, Lord,
You turned water into wine.

In my family relations
And the routine of the day;
In my work around the house, Lord,
And as problems come my way;
When family isn't easy
And relations cause me pain;
When joys I was expecting
Disappear beneath the strain;
When "Neighbours" seems familiar
As if I've been there before;
When sleep seems far from easy

And questions loom galore;
When I don't know how to cope, Lord,
And I cry out: "Heavens above!"
Then like water into wine, Lord,
The ordinary troubles
Melt in effervescent love.
You come to me to strengthen,
You're with me all the time;
And the water of my home life
You're transforming into wine.

Water into wine, Lord,
New life You will provide.
Water into wine, Lord,
You turn water into wine.

I sit in church on Sundays
On the comfortable pews;
Arriving very early
I sometimes sit and muse.
You said Your church was people
Related by Your love,
We're equally important
And for You we are to live.
We're ordinary folk, Lord,
With faith and questions, too,
But we witness to Your Kingdom,
And this You call us to.
You've trusted us to witness
To your truth and love and grace,
And the loveliness of Jesus
Should be seen in every face.
Our hands are Yours to serve, Lord,
Our lips are Yours to speak,
Our love is Yours to care, Lord,
Each day of every week.
We're like ordinary water

From the spring or from the rain,
Who can become the wine of heaven
Refreshing others in Your name.

Water into wine, Lord,
New life You will provide.
Water into wine, Lord,
You turn water into wine.

I remember how You met, Lord,
For supper with Your friends;
'Twas was then You took a cup, Lord,
Offering love that never ends.
You took it in Your hands, Lord,
Transforming it with love.
And offered it to us, Lord,
A feast from heaven above.
In a house out at Emmaus
Broken bread transformed that place,
And a simple kitchen table
Was the alter of Your grace.
With ordinary symbols
You bid us come and dine,
And the water of our future
Becomes a rich red wine.

Water into wine, Lord,
New life You will provide,
Water into wine, Lord,
You turn water into wine.

ANOINTING
(A Meditation)

Secretly, silently, she came,
A woman, extravagant with love.
Changed and transformed by the Master,
Saved to begin again.
What could she bring to express her gratitude?
What could she do to show how deeply she loved?
Her most precious jar of perfume
Sat conspicuously on her table
Waiting the day when the most important
Event in her life occurred,
When someone unquestionably special
Accepted her.

But His acceptance was different.
The holy, perfect Son of God accepted her
When others counted her as refuse
On the scrap heap of a fallen world.
Unacceptable, but accepted
She came, secretly, silently,
A woman changed by the extravagance of love.
Unobtrusively she entered with her precious jar,
Then broke it open to liberate a fragrance
No one could fail to notice,
And eyes turned to see her
Anoint the head of Jesus
In an extravagance of love.
What waste! Such economic nonsense!
Look at the alternatives of hope
If perfume is converted into money.
But this not about support,
It is about sacrifice.
This is not an act of personal emotion,
But a great proclamation for all time

Of the extravagance of love.
For this is the preparation of a body for burial,
A body sacrificed to save the world
Because of an extravagance of love
Flowing from the heart of God
In Jesus – to all of us.

ANOINTED
(Based on St. Luke)

Secretly, silently I came,
My face hidden beneath my hood;
Hidden from the gaze of those who
Judged me – a woman of ill repute,
The town's prostitute.

But secretly, silently I came
To the home of a holy man
Who would have sent me packing
Had he recognised me
For who and what I was.

But Simon, the Pharisee, didn't know.
No-one could have known about the truth
And love that touched my heart
From the preacher from Nazareth,
The gracious Rabbi, Jesus.

I'd known so many men before
But this man changed my life;
His words had reached my ears and
Penetrated deep within my heart;
Life *could* be different – clean and new.

So secretly, silently I came,
And through the open door
I entered the crowded room
Where people, stretched on couches,
Wined and dined with their holy host.

Secretly, silently I crept so close
Until I knelt beside this man
And wept such tears of love
They drenched His naked feet –
And His eyes met mine.

My loosened hair became
The cloth to wipe my tears,
And from my neck I took perfume
To anoint those feet, not knowing that one day
They would bare the marks of nails.

But Simon the holy Pharisee,
Poured out his scorn and indignation,
And then, my Jesus, showed how his host had failed;
No foot washing or kiss of welcome,
No sweet ointment for His brow.

And then my Jesus told a story
About two debtors, one who owed so much
And the other just a little.
Both debts were cancelled by the master,
But which one will love him most?

"The one who received the greatest generosity
Of forgiveness I suppose", Simon said.
Then Jesus looked at me,
And in front of everyone, He said
"Your sins are forgiven."

Now I could "go in peace".
Words I had heard and had believed,
So rich in their assurance.
Our God will never write us off;
In Jesus He offers a new beginning.

HANDS

I looked upon the gentle hands
Laid on a small child's head.
"God bless and keep both you and your mum",
The man with the gentle hands said.

I looked upon the healing hands
Raising a little girl, thought dead.
"Arise little girl, and come and eat",
The man with the healing hands said.

I looked upon the serving hands
Washing feet, a task to dread.
"I give you an example to serve one another",
The man with the serving hands said.

I looked upon the sharing hands
Feeding a hungry crowd with bread.
"Make the people sit down upon the green grass",
The man with the sharing hands said.

I looked upon the saving hands
Of a man nailed high 'till dead.
"Father, forgive them, they don't understand",
The man with the saving hands said.

Gentle, healing, serving, sharing -
Hands which by love are led.
But pierced, bloodstained, saving hands?
God was speaking: "I love you", He said.

(Author's Note:
Our hands can reveal so much about us. My father's hands were
rough because of the years he spent working with timber, but they
were hands that blessed and cared and served. That pointed me to
think of the hands of Jesus, who probably worked as a carpenter in
his younger days, and how those same hands revealed so much
tenderness and love.)

The
Way
of
the
Cross

A PALM SUNDAY POEM

The Pilgrim way to Passover
Is filled with palms and songs,
From town and cities near and far
Great crowds the city throng.

To Temple courts come worshippers
With joyful celebration,
Remembering their deliverance,
God's act of great salvation.

But then amidst the festival
The Prince of Peace draws near
Upon a village donkey
And the crowds begin to cheer.

"Hosanna!" loud "Hosanna!"
With joyful celebration,
"Is this the King the prophets said
Would bring again salvation?"

With palms and cloaks they strew His way
While others plot and plan;
The promise now is sacrifice
For this, the Son of Man.

HOSANNA!

"Hosanna" shouts and waving palms;
Crowds acclaim, cheers, joy and praise;
Temple cleansing whips and cords;
Confrontation, challenge, conspiracy.
Then washing feet, an upper room,
Bread and Wine, a meal with friends;
A prayer, a protest,
Garden and Kiss;
A king, a governor,
Thorny crown
And wooden cross;
A hill, a cry;
Forgiveness;
Paradise;
Tears;
Silence ...

... Silence
Daybreak
Awakening hope
An empty grave
A gardener midst the tears;
A voice, a name.
Alive! Alive! Renewed! Alive!
Faith wakened; hope restored.
Conversation on a lonely road;
Bread broken and eyes opened.
New life! New purpose! Now for glory!

WHO ARE YOU JESUS?
(A Meditation)

Who are you, Jesus?

Born a Jew,
you played in the streets of Nazareth;
walked through the lanes of Galilee;
reached out to the blind and lame;
those with mental illness and those with leprosy.

You had meals with people many hated and despised;
and you set them free to live new lives.

Jesus, your words brought comfort and challenge;
your touch brought healing and acceptance;
your presence brought peace to many and disturbed others.

Who are you, Jesus, with such authority,
compassion, the capacity to welcome all and reject none.

Who are you Jesus that you should live like us;
feel pain;
be upset;
be rejected;
and yet you loved those who did not deserve it.

Could you possibly be God?

The Christ - the Messiah - a King?

Kings have kingdoms, armies, defences, boundaries of authority.

But where is your kingdom?

You turned down the idea of conquering nations when you worked things out in the desert.

Who are you Jesus that you now speak of
suffering, rejection, death?

Could your kingdom come through sacrifice?
Could your greatness be in perfect love?

Something deep inside says:
"YOU ARE THE CHRIST - in majesty and humility"
and you will never give up on me.

REMEMBERED

Servants, soldiers, stirrers,
All clustered in a courtyard
Round a fire.
Shadows of authority dramatically dancing in the firelight
On the wall of the High Priest's house.
Conversation, speculation, condemnation,
All reaching conclusions in advance of truth.
What happens now?
They say he was arrested for blasphemy.
Rumour has it, a friend betrayed him.
The Rabbi from Galilee must answer now
To the High Priest
And the might of Rome.
Don't forget Pilate. Don't forget the Governor.
He has the power of life and death.

People look around
Recognising faces in the firelight,
Questioning: "What happens now?"
Hidden in the shadows stands a man,
His identity concealed by darkness,
Until the firelight illuminates the truth,
And a servant girl is sure she knows him.

"This man was with Jesus."
"I do not know him."
"You are a disciple of Jesus."
"I do not know him."
"You must know him. You come from Galilee, too."
"I do not know him!"

A door opens; a cock crows,
Jesus stands, eyes full of sadness,
(pause)
And Peter remembers.

How easy it is to confess our faith
When we are amongst friends,
Like Peter at Caesarea Philippi.
"You are the Christ, the Son of the Living God!"
How hard it is to honour Christ
When faced with reality
On the stage of life.
The eyes of Jesus see us as we are,
And we remember our failures.
Faith and failure are such close opponents,
But divided by a deep chasm.
Thank God that Jesus remembers failure
In order to redeem it.

GOOD FRIDAY

(At the beginning of the year we took down the Christmas tree. Stripped of its branches, the main stem was divided in order to make from it a cross. That cross stood in a suitable support draped with green cloth. Between the singing of hymns about the Passion, the story was told in brief simplicity, supported by sounds and visual aids. This link story is for three voices.)

The three voices are defined by A, B and C

A: Betrayed.

B: Denied.

C: Condemned to die.

A: Who shall I release to you? Jesus or Barabbas?

B: Give us Barabbas!

A: What shall I do with Jesus? Asked Pilate.

C: Crucify him! Crucify him!

A: How they clamoured for his death!

B: And Pilate washed his hands.

C: In the palace grounds they stripped him.

A: Mocked him.

B: Whipped him.

(SOUND OF WHIPPING)

C: Long live the King of the Jews!

A: They took a stick and hit him over the head.

B: And then, in mockery, dressed him in a purple robe.

C: Led away through the crowded streets, he came to Calvary, and there they hung him on a cross.

(PURPLE CLOTH IS DRAPED OVER THE ARMS OF THE CROSS)

A: His hands were pierced with nails.

(NAILS ARE HUNG FROM THE CROSS)

B: He was wounded for our transgressions.
C: And his brow was pierced with a crown of sharp thorns.

(A THORNY CROWN IS PLACED ON THE CROSS)

A: Is it nothing to you, all you that pass by?
    Was there ever such sorrow like His sorrow?

SPONGE

(This poem was written as a challenge while doing a creative writing evening with some Methsoc students. Various objects had been placed on a table. Members of the group were invited to take one and use it to write something creative. I was left with an ordinary sponge.)

Soaked in vinegar, oozing wet
With Fairy Liquid froth beset,
A yellow sponge is what you are
Poised to squelch upon my car.

Soaked in vinegar, lifted up,
No hand to hold a bitter cup;
The answer to the cry, "I thirst!",
As hands feel evil at its worst.

Freshly dipped in running brook,
Water of life for you I look;
Squeeze the sponge upon my brow,
Water of life refresh me now.

Love is a sponge that soaks up pain;
Gives and forgives again and again.

MY SON! MY SON!

(In this meditation Mary, the Mother of Jesus is speaking as she stands near the cross with all her feelings and questions. It was inspired by a visit to Oberammergau for a performance of the famous Passion Play.)

Why have they done this to you, Jesus?
Nailed your hands to a tree of death;
Shouted your "Hosannas"
Then clamoured for a cross.

Why have they done this to you, Jesus?
Priests conspiring; Pilate appeasing;
Soldiers mocking; Disciples fleeing;
Leaving you to scream your agony of forsakenness.

Why, Jesus? Why such futile sacrifice
When the world is desperate for a Saviour?

You came into the world with cries of pain,
The pain of birth before the manger,
You laughed and cried, played in the street,
Went to school, learned a trade,
Lived in a family;
You were one of us.

Then came the time for letting go,
Called, confirmed, commissioned by your Father.
Lake shores and country lanes,
Homes and open hills
Were the venues for your ministry;
Places where all were welcome
And there were no barriers to faith.
Some came with questions mingled with mixed motives;
Others curious, longing, needing, hoping.
Multitudes hung upon your words as

Compassion, healing, mercy, invited new beginnings.
You <u>did</u> come to seek and save!
You came to reconcile a fallen world to God
And bring God's promised Kingdom of harmony and peace.

But why a cross - a crown - a contemptible Calvary death?
My Son! My Son!
Let me hear your voice and understand
The reason for your bleeding sacrifice.
Forgive! You said "Forgive"?
You plead with God for those who betray,
deny, despise and reject you?
"Today with me in Paradise"?
You promise life eternal to a thief who knows he's wrong and now regrets it?

From the cross you declare the endless possibility
Of love and grace for those who cause you pain.

My Son! My Son!
Once my arms encircled you;
Now your arms encircle the world
And your wounds are the marks of love that heals.

Why this, Jesus? Why a cross?
I think I am beginning to understand.
It is the place where the hurt of the world
Is confronted with the perfect love of God
And your death promises resurrection.

FORGIVENESS

Forgiveness is an outstretched hand
To heal the brokenness of years
Marred by the lingering bitterness
Of wounds unhealed.

Forgiveness is a word of love
Which dissolves the memory of past hurts
In streams of grace, and seeks
To give a new beginning.

Forgiveness is a willingness to
Leave behind a history of pain
And give another chance for love
Until it hurts with hope.

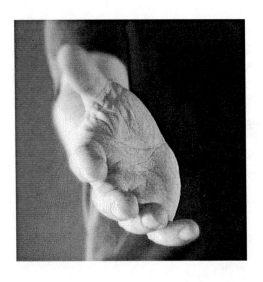

EASTER

When the sunrise bathes the earth in pure new light
And blackbirds sing spring songs of joy;
When the dead black earth of winter is greened with shoots of life,
An Easter world of glorious new creation now is born.

When a heavy stone that guards a dead man's tomb is moved,
And angels speak of resurrection life;
When hands, with prints of love, break bread with friends,
An Easter future for a broken world is born.

When the story of a risen Lord is told, and praise rings out from chapel doors;
When daybreak dawns within my heart, and a
Saviour speaks my name,
An Easter faith amidst a sea of doubts is born.

He whom God has raised now raises me,
And I, too, am now reborn.

Travelling On

LORD, IMMERSE ME IN THE WORLD
Meditation

Lord, immerse me in the world,
But keep me true.
Let my integrity of faith and love,
Of noble vision and high ideals,
Keep me in tune with heaven
Amidst the discord of our world.
Let my life be a song of truth
That will keep on being sung
Until it joins a chorus of harmonious voices,
A choir to your glory.

Lord, immerse me in the world,
A candle's flickering flame
In a world of darkness.
Let my light be pure and warm,
A flame of hope and honour,
Until the darkness flees and
The world is bathed in glory.

Lord, immerse me in the world,
A pinch of salt
To purify intentions;
To preserve the best of goodness;
To bring new meaning to community;
To make a difference with love.
Dissolve me in the pool of life's experiences
Until the kingdoms of this world
Become the kingdom of Your glory.

ANGER

(A poem composed while attending a Lent Workshop on "anger")

When the bomber blasts the Baghdad street,
And children scream midst streams of blood;
When hatred and despair claw darkened skies,
And eyes blaze red with anger and revenge;
Where are you, God?

When the multi-national companies
Clasp profits which delight exchanges,
While Aids victims cry out for possibilities of hope,
And a generation's potential lies in ruins;
Where are you God?

When dollar bills fly like cartons of confetti
Into accounts of those with arsenals of arms;
While families look for shelter, food and care,
And long for seeds of justice to be sown;
Where are you, God?

When the asylum seeker knocks upon the door
Of entry to a country where freedom spells a future,
And prejudice and fear are spread
In hostile leaflets of discrimination;
Where are you, God?

When people preferred a murderer and a thief
To a man of love and peace and life,
And hands which healed and blessed and served
Were torn to shreds by nails of evil and of fear,
Where were you, God?

Child, I am there in the suffering and the pain;
There in the hopelessness and need;
There in the cries for love which echo round the world;
There in the hands of sacrifice.
Have you not seen me?

Let your anger become the passion of my loving
And your kindness be the grace of my presence.
Open your heart and extend your hands
And then I shall be recognised,
For I am where you are.

FORGIVENESS DILEMMA
Meditation

(First presented at a conference on "abuse".
Each verse represents a different character.)

Who am I?
Battered, bruised, broken by pain;
Pain in my limbs; pain in my heart;
Afraid to scream, to shout, to speak;
Silenced by fear;
Locked into my prison of solitude;
Wet with tears of unshared hurt; feeling the weight of guilt,
but wanting to plead "not guilty".
A child, waiting for love,
waiting for liberty, waiting for healing.

Who am I?
Battered, bruised, broken by pain;
The pain of my feelings, faults and failures;
The guilt of hurt inflicted by my own appetite for self-
gratification, power, control;
The manipulative me, disguising lust with love;
The divided me, capable of the highest good and the deepest
evil.
"The good that I would do, I don't do.
The evil that I don't want to do, that I do.
Who will deliver me from this body of death."

Who am I?
Watching, knowing, but denying.
A witness to hidden truth,
A partner in silenced suffering,
Comforting, but condoning;
Living with silence which prolongs the hurt;
Wanting to see change, but denying reality;
Broken by fear.
Who am I?
Accepting, loving, caring;
healing abuse with love;
Helping forgiveness to grow inside;
to heal the brokenness of fear
and somehow unlock the door that leads to freedom.
Accepting, loving caring, listening to the unacceptable;
Knowing that grace is free undeserved love,
But recognising that protection may be the most loving thing to do;
Protection for those who have been hurt;
Protection for those who have caused hurt.
Healing love and forgiveness should have no boundaries;
But sometimes love and forgiveness can only heal when
we are protected from ourselves.

WORDS ARE EASY

It's easy to say "Happy Birthday"
To a colleague at work on the day,
But then undermine her position,
Determined to get your own way.

It's easy to say "May God bless you"
To a lonely neighbour in need;
But never show practical kindness,
For it's just too much trouble to heed.

It's easy to say "Peace be with you"
Before the communion bread;
Then, in the street, keep your distance,
Remembering something once said.

It's easy to say "How I love you"
In an intimate moment of life;
But a single moment of passion
Doesn't heal all the anger and strife.

It's easy to say "I forgive you"
And still hold a grudge in your heart.
Unless you let go of the issue
There never will be a fresh start.

Sometimes words that we speak are easy,
An outward expression of good.
But what are we like on the inside?
That truth is open to God.

FROM DAWN TILL DUSK
Meditation and Prayer

(Written as a voice-over for a friend's film shot off the coast of mid Wales.)

As the silent glow of sunrise
Horizons the dawn,
The shrill calls of seabirds
Waken the new day with joyful expectation.
A new beginning is being born
With immanent possibilities.

> *God of majesty and mystery,*
> *Creator and Giver of life;*
> *The Beginning and the End;*
> *With all creation we honour You*
> *And pledge the life of this new day.*

As the restless sea,
Sometimes gentle, sometimes strong,
With changing tides and moods,
Smooth sand cuts the rocky coast,
So the sea of life, sometimes gentle,
Sometimes rough and strong,
Smooths and shapes our character.

> *Lord we live in Your world*
> *Touched by all its experiences,*
> *But sustained by Your love.*
> *Shape our character with Your gentle kindness*
> *And Your powerful strength.*

As hidden sounds of joy
Rise from beneath the waves,
Dolphins leap and dive
To celebrate with anticipation
The promise each new day brings.

Lord, You have given us freedom
To be, to live;
A gift to be embraced.
As creatures call out to each other,
We call out to you.
Help us to hear Your voice
And listen to each other
That we may better understand each other's dreams
And create the harmony which
characterises Your Kingdom.

When we face the storms,
And we are battered and blown,
You stretch out Your hand
Like a loving Father
To keep us safe and secure.

Lord, You are our constant
Companion and friend,
From dawn till dusk
You share each moment;
And when we truly rest in You,
Whose love never fails,
May we know that all,
All, all will be well.

A PRAYER WHEN
THE GOING IS TOUGH

As we walk in the wilderness,
Show us a flower of beauty,
Fragrant and colourful.
As we walk in the darkness,
Grant us a candle of hope
To illuminate the future.
As we are covered with sombre clouds,
Show us a rainbow to lift our spirit.
As we feel lost and alone,
Take our hands and
Warm them with your love.

AUTUMN LEAVES

Autumn leaves, orange, yellow, reddish brown,
Gently falling to the ground
With a rustic carpet,
Ending the story of creation for another year,
Until new days are born,
After the dark silence of a winter sleep.

Autumn leaves, blown by the breeze
Into rustic heaps on pavements
All the way to school;
Kicked and crushed and trampled by a thousand feet,
As if their beauty counts for nothing any more.

But then one loving hand reaches down
To take a single golden leaf,
And gently smoothing its crumpled, trampled form,
Places it between the pages of a book,
There to be held safe for ever;
A life remembered in God's book of life,
Whose beauty never dies.

Autumn leaves, orange, yellow, reddish brown,
Gently covering the ground
With a rustic carpet;
There, beneath the trees, to feed the earth
With next year's nourishment,
In readiness for Spring.
Each leaf a life that has a future still,
To help new generations come to life
With a beauty nurtured by past years.

A season rich in colour and alive with fruit;
Grapes gathered into a stone pit,
Waiting for a thousand feet
To trample fruit into a rich, red wine.
Only through pain is so much beauty born;
Only through dying is new life begun.

No leaf lies useless on the ground;
It nourishes tomorrow's life.
No fruit is trodden under foot for nothing;
It oozes with the promise of new wine.

Between the pages of the Book of Life
Are many leaves,
Never forgotten,
And for ever loved.

LET THERE BE LIGHT!

(Linking together creation with new creation in Christ, this piece was originally written as an accompaniment to music and dance.)

"Let there be light", God said,
And from the dazzling birth of creation
Came a flood of beauty, colour and of life
That cascaded through the galaxies;
That rainbowed the world;
That dazzled the oceans;
And greened the earth.

Light shone, and a world dawned,
Love was born
And eyes shone with happiness and hope.
Each human life intended to become
A star of beauty and of love
To bathe the earth in reflected glory,
Dancing through the world in the image of the creator.

But light has also shown us truth,
A truth about ourselves, our world,
And we have marred the image of His loveliness
And given birth to a new darkness of our own.

But light still shines
And seeks us for new birth,
And makes us promises of love
We cannot ever deserve but only delight in.

When Jesus came, light danced through the world anew
And showed up the darkness.
Darkness was crucified
And love rose up triumphant
Dance on, Light of the World!
Dance on in every place and time!
Dance on, beauty and love!
Dance on in us
For that will be true blessedness.

ONE LIFE, ONE CANDLE

One life, one candle, burning in a world
Crying out for love, longing for peace.
A world nailed to history by violence and fear,
Where love is pierced by pain,
Where hope lies buried in the rubble
Of ignorance and cruelty,
Where joy is a dream in the eyes of a child.
For such a world
God sent the Light of the World, Jesus Christ,
To shine in the darkness with pure and holy love.

Put the candle of your life to Him today
And touch the flame of love
That you may shine out His glory
And be aglow with His life.

One lifetime to take the candle of our life
And let it touch the flame of the Light of the World
And become in us, a glow of love,
And through us, a beam of hope.

One lifetime to let Jesus Christ
Shine in us and heal all our failures
And then through us to bring healing to a hurting world.

Look upwards to see the One who loves you
And holds you in His heart.

Look inwards to see the good that can be deepened
And the faults that can be changed.

Look outwards and see His light shine through you
To bless the lives of all you meet.

One life, One Candle – yours and mine.
But such is the power of light and love
That comes from Christ
That the darkness cannot put it out.
Oh, that we all might catch the flame.

MOORLEYS
Print & Publishing

As a well established publisher we add several new titles to our list each year. We also undertake private publications and commissioned works.

Our range includes

Books of Verse
Devotional Poetry
Recitations for Children
Humorous Monologues

Drama
Bible Plays
Sketches
Christmas, Passiontide,
Easter & Harvest Plays
Demonstrations

Resource Books
Assembly Material
Easy Use Music Books for Piano and Keyboard
Children's Addresses
Prayers
Worship & Preaching
Books for Speakers

Activity Books
Quizzes & Puzzles

Church Stationery
Notice Books & Cradle Roll Certificates

Associated Lists and Imprints
Cliff College Publishing
Nimbus Press
MET (Headway)
Social Work Christian Fellowship

For up to date news, special offers & information on our full list of titles, please visit our website at www.moorleys.co.uk

Alternatively send a stamped addressed C5 envelope for our current catalogue, or consult your local Christian Bookshop, who will either stock or be able to obtain our titles.